SPIRITUAL WISDOM
FOR
MONEY MANAGEMENT

Preface

Money is not merely currency; it is a visible form of the invisible energy that sustains life. Just as the body requires food, shelter, clothing, rest, and recreation, and just as the heart longs for companionship and love, so too does the soul seek an environment free from poverty and limitation, wherein it may flower fully. To live wholly—body, mind, and spirit—man must learn to handle money with wisdom.

Yet, the world's relentless pursuit of money often springs not from joy, but from an inner emptiness. In trying to fill that void with possessions and power, one distances oneself from true fulfillment. Only a rare soul dares to gaze into that emptiness through meditation, discovering within it a reservoir of unshakable joy. In that awakening, money ceases to be an obsession and becomes instead a tool—an instrument for service, harmony, and circulation of life-energy.

Earning wealth and walking the spiritual path are not contradictory. Indeed, when money is managed through the lens of dharma, it ceases to be hoarded out of fear and begins to flow with purpose. By giving freely, without attachment, we align ourselves with the great cosmic law that life rewards us in proportion to our contribution.

This book, Spiritual Wisdom for Money Management, offers you simple yet profound insights into the subtle laws that govern abundance. It is not merely about wealth—it is about right relationship with wealth. May these pages inspire you to treat money not as a master to be feared, nor as a prize to be chased, but as a co-creator of higher living.

When handled with awareness, money supports prosperity, nurtures love, and helps us walk steadily toward the ultimate treasure—happiness rooted in the Self.

Dhyāna Ratna S.K. Rajan
Chairman
Soulfull Federation Trust®

Contents

General Principles of Money

1. Born in poverty:

   i) He does not take trouble to earn money as he is lazy.

   ii) He is one who has only ignored physical conditions and spent all his energy in building castles in the air.

2. Wealth is possessed according to the past or present energies of labor or thought that he possesses now or possessed in the past.

3. Money is obtained due to previous work or effort.

4. Right or wrong use of money will determine if one will enjoy or suffer with lot of money.

5. Money is the closest companion of those who chase it. But there is no assurance of normal health and the person dies a discontented man.

6. He may or may not make proper use of it. Neglect of his children, insanity, and lack of a person to inherit the wealth are common among the idle, luxurious offspring of the rich and idle. Money then becomes a curse.

7. Those who are unscrupulous and dishonest in life and in business will find they are legalized robbers Hence they will find their true expression later, when they are externalized.

8. They are born as rogues or cheats and suffer from birth. If he was a thief, he is marked and outlawed, convicted, and caged. He has to pay for all his wrongdoings.

9. Those who make ostentatious use or misuse money will realize the value of money and struggle through poverty.

10. Properly acquired wealth gives proper physical conditions for comfort, enjoyment and work for self and others.

11. One who inherits money from affluent parents or has earned it through right thought and actions will not face accident of wealth or of inheritance.

12. The universal law of magnetic attraction states that if one works with love, he can pursue his life until they lead him into a labor of love.

Laws of Manifestation

Essential Laws that Govern Manifestation of Money

1. LAW OF KARMA

This law emphasizes "as you sow, so you shall reap." essentially, it suggests that our actions, both in this lifetime and previous ones, comes with consequences that we must face. All religions of the East view the law of Karma, as a cosmic mechanism of balance ...what goes around, come around...and they recommend doing wholesome actions of body, speech, and mind to ensure that one experiences in the here and hereafter. This law is based on the truth of our "inter-connection".

2. LAW OF ATTRACTION

This law says that if we have a clear intention, precisely that will manifest in our experience if we allow it to. In short it means " Like attracts like "Each of us is a magnet attracting to us all things, via the signal that we keep emitting throughout thoughts and feelings.

3. LAW OF ABUNDANCE

Money, being neutral-it's energy and attitude towards it that create 'happy' or 'unhappy money. 'The happy money philosophy teaches and leads to not just a feeling of abundance, but actual abundance.

A person with a mindset of abundance has the belief that his mind is a reservoir of new ideas that paves the way for creation of an eternal spring from which flows all wealth, success, fulfillment, and accomplishment. Abundance comes in two forms—visible and invisible. Visible abundance includes money and tangible assets, while invisible abundance comprises values, trust, friendship, love, generosity, care, and kindness. While tangible assets are important, invisible assets are enriching and invaluable.

4. LAW OF GIVING

The 'Law of Giving 'states that as money is like blood, it must be allowed to circulate. In order to grow it must flow. Hence the important principle is that that this "life energy" must be allowed and encouraged to circulate if it has to keep coming to us. We may practice the habit of giving away a portion of our income without condition and strings attached. The principles of this law are followed in no small measure by bountiful Nature that gives humanity in abundance—grass, flowers, trees, etc.

5. LAW OF MONEY MYSTIQUE

The secret of money energy is that the green energy of money travels in a magnetic circle. When we let go of the money, it follows as an invisible circle of pure and powerful energy which will return to you in multiplied form. The rules relating to the law states that when we comprehend it, believe in it and practice it, the money that is given with good intentions, will not only return to you; it will return 3-fold or, 4-fold from an unexpected source.

Spiritual Laws

Spirituality And Money

Whether money goes with spirituality or not has been a subject of discussion in man's mind from time immemorial but the conventional thinking amongst people in general is that money and spirituality do not go together. According to Sri Aurobindo, "It is quite possible for a man to do business and make money and earn profits and yet be a spiritual man, practice Yoga and have inner life. "Spiritual masters see money as a symbol of creative energy. Money is exactly similar to the creative energy of the universe which is limitless and so is money. Our capacity to earn and spend money abundantly and in a wise manner is based on how we adapt ourselves to become a channel for it to flow through us. The tougher and more open our channel is, greater will be the flow through it. So, as Linda Goodman, puts it "As long as you cheerfully and willingly give away half of what you have, to the less fortunate, you need not be ashamed to be a millionaire or even a billionaire- because you have let go half, thereby allowing this 'Green Energy' to circulate. (Also, because you earned it by honest work).

Money has been described as the root of evil. Money, by itself is not evil, nor is it the path to happiness. Only the use of it and the means of creating it cause it to be categorized as evil or good.

Spirituality In Practice

What many of us are familiar with is spiritual religion that is not a part of spirituality, but a part of religion. Real spirituality is a revolutionary process that happens in your consciousness. When the revolution culminates successfully, the ego is replaced by a higher state of consciousness that is above and beyond ego. True spirituality involves attaining the goal of transformation of our consciousness irrespective of the religion to which we belong. When we experience a change of consciousness, our religious status will disappear. If, however, neither religion nor spirituality interest us, we do not have to bother, as what is needed is inner development. What we have is two kinds of development -interior development and amazing exterior development. For achieving this state, a balance between spirituality and materialism i.e. the inside and outside is absolutely essential.

Earning money and being a spiritual person at the same time are not mutually exclusive. A person who is rich need not feel a sense of guilt merely because many lack wealth and are in poverty. However, there are some general rules to be followed in creating, managing, and using wealth which becomes important if we have to conserve wealth.

Three Reasons that Encourage Earning Money

1. The important reason for getting employed is to earn your daily bread

2. To become a person of affluence

3. To ensure that your respectability in society is maintained through exercising your potential to earn.

Persons who have inherited wealth from forefathers work to preserve and retain inherited fortune and to have a standing in society.

The Spiritual Principle of Money and Its Management

- Unity of Existence

    o All wealth and resources are manifestations of the One Supreme Substance.

    o Money, rightly viewed, is not separate from Spirit but a tool for self-unfolding.

- Money as a Means, Not an End

    o To develop body, mind, and soul, one needs resources.

    o Money provides access to food, shelter, education, beauty, art, and companionship— each vital for wholeness.

- Right to Prosperity

    o Every being has an inborn right to growth and abundance.

    o True life means full expression of body, intellect, and spirit— poverty stifles this divine potential.

- Nature's Law of Growth

  o Contentment with too little is against the purpose of life.

  o Nature intends expansion; abundance is the rightful condition of man.

- Holistic Living Requires Balance

  o To live fully:

    — The body needs nourishment, rest, and comfort.

    — The mind needs study, travel, and intellectual exchange.

    — The soul needs love, giving, and service.

  o Denying one dimension weakens the others.

- Money as an Instrument of Love

  o Love expresses itself most naturally through giving and sharing.

  o A person without means cannot fulfill duties to family, society, or even to the Universe fully.

- Science of Money Management

  o Wealth must be pursued wisely, not greedily, through discipline and responsibility.

  o Managing money is managing one's dharma— it aligns personal growth with service to the Divine.

- Spiritual Duty of Wealth

  - o To neglect the principle of wise wealth creation and management is to deny potential that we possess.

  - o By unfolding oneself through rightful prosperity, one serves family, community, and the Supreme.

In essence: Money is not to be shunned, nor worshiped, but revered as a sacred instrument of self- realization, service, and the blossoming of life's higher purposes When we unite spiritual wisdom with practical discipline, we are ensuring that money becomes a servant of the soul and not its master.

Management—Dos & Donts

Dos and Don'ts for the Seeker of Truth

Do's – The Path of Dharma in Money

- Earn righteously (Dharma-Ārjana): Seek wealth only through honest work, fair trade, and rightful means.

- Meet genuine needs first: Use money for food, clothing, shelter, health, and education – essentials for life and dharmic living.

- Aim for independence, not indulgence: Let money serve your freedom of mind and body, not bind you to endless desires.

- Use wealth for higher purpose: Direct surplus wealth towards service, charity, education, and the upliftment of society.

- Exercise contentment (Santosha): Train the mind to remain satisfied with "enough" rather than chasing "more."

- Safeguard family and dependents: Provide with responsibility, but do not spoil children with excess money or neglect them with indifference.

- Learn from reversals: If money is lost, see it as destiny's training to develop humility, sympathy, and balance.

- Respect inheritance as earned karma: Treat inherited wealth which is earned through good karma in past lives, as sacred responsibility, to be preserved and shared with integrity.

- Value simplicity: The less dependent you are on luxury, the freer and more fearless your spirit becomes.

- Keep honesty inviolable: In every financial act, let truth be the currency and conscience be the banker.

DON'TS – The Pitfalls of Greed

- Do not worship money as a god: Wealth is a servant, never the master.

- Do not exploit others: Avoid earning through deceit, injustice, or exploitation.

- Do not live for luxury and display: Showcasing riches only breeds vanity, rivalry, jealousy, and sorrow.

- Do not neglect dependents: Riches lose their worth if family bonds are broken through negligence or when dependents are neglected.

- Do not chase endless accumulation: Beyond needs, the craving for "more" brings restlessness, disease, and dissatisfaction.

- Do not ignore inner wealth: Money cannot purchase love, health, wisdom, or peace of mind.

- Do not despise poverty: To be born in poverty is not shameful; indolence and lack of effort are.

- Do not misuse inheritance: Squandering ancestral wealth invites degeneration and bondage.

- Do not forget destiny's law: Misuse of wealth leads to future want; right use leads to true independence.

- Do not lose balance: Let not money blind the heart to truth, compassion, and spiritual growth.

Wealth and Work

In his book '30 Lessons for Living', gerontologist Karl Pillemer interviewed a thousand elderly citizens looking for the most important lessons they learned from decades of life experience.

He wrote:

- No one—not a single person out of a thousand -said that to be happy you should try to work as hard as you can to make money to buy the things you want.

- No one—not a single person—said it is important to be at least as wealthy as the people around you, and if you have more than they do, it is real success

- No one—not a single person—said you should choose your work based on your desired future earning power.

What they really valued were:

Quality friendships, being part of something bigger than themselves, and spending quality, unstructured time with their children.

"Your kids do not want your money (or what your money buys) anywhere near as much as they want you. Specifically, they want you with them."

Money Magnet

Money-Features

Money is magnetic energy. You are a magnet attracting to all things, via the signal you are emitting through your thoughts and feelings.

Money-Treatment

- The treatment of money is related to the effects that it causes on our relationships and our health.

- As money is energy, - flow with it

- Money creates relationships-so, love it

- Money determines health- so, glow with it.

Money Magnet

To become a money magnet i.e.to be able to attract money in this lifetime, certain areas need to be given adequate attention, viz.

1. The Spiritual laws that determine our actions particularly in the context of our actions in the present and in the past insofar as spiritual discipline is concerned.

2. Every single relationship you have reflects how you feel inside about you since you are a magnet

attracting to you all things, via your thoughts and feelings.

3. Being loving for what you own and possess and feeling grateful to the Universe for your present condition makes you happy. Disease is the body's way of giving you feedback that you are not loving and grateful.

Action Points to Become a Powerful Money Magnet

1. Be clear about how much money you require.

2. Speak, act and think from the mindset of being wealthy now.

3. Do not speak or think of the lack of money even for a second.

4. Be grateful for the money you have. Appreciate it as you touch it.

5. Feel wealthy and try to feel that way, always.

6. Affirm to yourself everyday that you have an abundance of money and that it comes to you effortlessly.

7. Appreciate all the riches around you, including the riches of others. Look for wealth wherever you go and appreciate it.

8. Be certain that money is coming to you.

9. Love yourself and know that you are deserving and worthy of an abundance of money.

10. Remind yourself everyday that you are a money magnet and ask yourself often during the day – "am I attracting money now or pushing it away with my thoughts?"

11. Always, always pay yourself first from your wage, and then pay your creditors. [in that single act, you are telling the universe that you are worthy and deserving of more]

12. Do whatever it takes to feel good. The emotions of joy and happiness are powerful money magnets. Be happy now!

13. Money or wealth is a mindset. Money is literally attracted to you or repelled from you. It's all about how you think.

Relationships

14. Focus on wonderful qualities in every person.

15. Do not blame or criticize anyone.

16. Set an intention that you're going to see the best in everything and everyone.

17. Get your attention off those things in others that don't make you feel good.

18. Make your happiness the number one thing in your life.

19. Do not expect others to behave in a way you want, so you will be happy. Know that – you alone control your happiness and it's a choice.

19. Love and respect yourself completely.

20. Know that you're perfect right now.

Health

21. You're a magnet attracting to you all things, via the signal you are emitting through your thoughts and feelings.

22. Disease is a body's way of giving you a feedback.

23. See yourself as completely well in your mind.

24. Do not speak of your illness or disease with others.

25. Visualize yourself being in a completely perfect state of health.

26. Be happy that in your state of happiness, your body is healing itself.

A mantra for the Money Mystique

"I've been broke, but I've never been poor. Being broke is temporary. Being poor is a state of mind."

—Mike Todd

Creative Spirituality

Creative Spirituality For Money Management

How Spirituality Provides Workable Solutions for Handling Money?

Cultivating a discipline in our lives especially through meditation will enable every one of us to take control of our own lives. According to Osho, -Meditation is such a powerful thing that one hour of meditation each day will help to develop our sense of belonging with the universe and thus live our lives with harmony, health and happiness.

1. Money as Creative Energy

    o   Spirituality views money not as mere currency but as a *symbol of universal creative energy*.

    o   When seekers open themselves as clear channels—free from fear, greed, or doubt—money flows naturally, just as cosmic energy does.

    o   Solution: Instead of chasing money anxiously, cultivate openness, self-trust, and creativity. This makes earning and spending more effortless.

2. Removing Inner Blocks

   o Lack of money mirrors inner blockages such as insecurity, guilt, or lack of self-worth.

   o Through meditation and spiritual discipline, seekers clear these blocks and restore their natural state of abundance.

   o Solution: Practice daily meditation to cleanse the mind and allow prosperity to manifest without resistance.

3. Rightful Use of Wealth

   o Spirituality insists that wealth carries responsibility. Money received is not only personal property but also society's trust.

   o Solution: Use wealth righteously—for self-care, for family's needs, and for the good of society. When wealth circulates with benevolence, it multiplies and returns in unseen ways.

4. Living with Harmony

   o Meditation brings clarity, reduces confusion, and strengthens one's sense of belonging to the universe.

   o This clarity helps seekers make wise financial decisions, free from compulsive desires or wasteful habits.

o Solution: Spend consciously, not impulsively; align purchases with genuine needs and values.

5. Integrity in Money Matters

o True spirituality demands integrity and courage in all dealings—including financial ones.

o Solution: Handle money truthfully, without deceit or exploitation. Honesty builds trust, which attracts more opportunities for wealth.

6. Perspective of Gratitude

o Whatever we use on earth is "rent" to Mother Earth. Gratitude ensures we give back in service, charity, or kindness.

o Solution: Cultivate gratitude; tithe a portion of earnings to noble causes as an offering to the Source of all abundance.

In short: *Spirituality transforms money from a problem into a flow of creative energy. Meditation clears inner obstacles, integrity guides its use, gratitude ensures its circulation, and benevolence multiplies it back. Meditate, earn righteously, spend wisely, share joyfully, and remain detached. This is the spiritual way to manage money.*

Practicing

To be enlightened is precisely to practice This is done through regular practice of meditation. Thereby even the art of decision-making becomes easy. While commenting on the wisdom of the ancient spiritual masters, leading spiritual gurus delve into the depths of the human mind and analyse why it cannot be integrated enough to make decisions about money management in our own lives. They also suggest meditation to integrate one's life - energy and make a person undivided and absolutely capable of managing any crisis in his life.

FAQs

What is the difference between 'happy money 'and 'unhappy money?

Money is neutral—it is energy and attitude towards it that create 'happy' or 'unhappy' money. The happy money philosophy teaches and leads to not just a feeling of abundance, but actual abundance. If you feel stuck, be open to other solutions. While happy money ideas aren't miracles, they can guide you towards more fulfilling outcomes. (a Zen approach in money management)

What is an abundance mindset?

Abundance comes in two forms----visible and invisible.

Visible abundance includes money and tangible assets, while invisible abundance comprises values, trust, friendship, love, generosity, care, and kindness. While tangible assets are important, invisible assets like family, compassion, love etc. are enriching and invaluable.

However, there are also invisible debts--- emotional burdens placed on others, often seen in children of wealthy parents. These children may lack confidence due to an overdose of visible assets but a deficit of love and emotional support. Pay attention to both invisible debts and assets. LIFE IS NOT EASY OR HAPPY ON A SHOE-STRING BUDGET.

THIS MAKES US STRIVE FOR ABUNDANCE IN OUR LIVES

Could you give three tips towards an abundance mindset?

Three basic tips would be:

- SAY -THANK YOU

When money comes in, say 'thank you' and when money goes out, thank it again.

- DO WHAT YOU LOVE

Follow your passion using your talents. If obstacles exist, embrace what you do with happiness and grace. Finding fulfilment in your work leads to satisfaction, and appreciation puts you in a "happy high."

- CHERISH BEAUTIFUL RELATIONSHIPS

Deep relationships reduce worries and enhance life. Rely on relationships rather than bank accounts, so even in tough times, friends will support you.

Is it possible to spiritually manifest wealth?

According to the principle of Manifestation, there is an intelligence and a power in all nature that is creative and responsive. This intelligence is amenable to suggestion from us. Examine your thoughts carefully. See if those thoughts are totally in harmony with your actions. Such thoughts, emotions and behavior are strong indicators of self-trust. When you trust in yourself, you are trusting in the universe at the same time. Practice of surrendering leads to acknowledging your fundamental richness. Thereby, you practice spiritual trust and also surrender your ego and all of its beliefs to a higher power. As the divine guidance is then always with you, you can literally confront yourself in a spirit of serenity. What you seek will then be attracted to you. This is the energy of manifesting, and it comes most frequently when the mind is quiet. It is the quiet mind that comes in contact with the truth.

What about resentment people feel when paying for taxes or medical bills?

Resentment around money is common because we feel like something is being taken away forcefully. But consider this: we don't have any grudges when we release waste from our bodies each morning. We accept it because we understand it's necessary for our health. Similarly, taxes and bills are essential for our comfort. They ensure that services like electricity, water and infrastructure continue to function. Resentment around legitimate payments is counterproductive and de- energizing. Instead, be grateful that these services are managed well, allowing you to live comfortably.

How do we know when we have enough money with us?

Even with Rs. 100 in your bank account, you can feel abundant. One reason we need not be afraid of inadequate money is that friends and close relatives will have money on whom we can rely for support in times of need. To combat greed, we should focus on the joy and satisfaction that comes from non-material wealth.

What are 'money wounds' and how can they be healed?

Money wounds are often the core issue behind an individual's financial abundance being blocked. These are imbibed and transmitted from our family in the form of limiting beliefs and hurt around them. Money wounds can create an individual's financial reality because the wound may centre around "I am not worthy enough to have more money." And this belief will make it hard to keep money flowing into your life. So, identify and be aware of beliefs or patterns around money. One way is to develop practice of appreciation. Once you appreciate money without malice or greed, money appreciates.

Quotations from Eminent Spiritual Masters

1. Jesus Christ

- "Seek ye the kingdom of God and his righteousness first; All else will be added unto you."

- "The seeker who bestows attention to following the path of righteous living will be the beneficiary of all that the life on earth can offer once he takes steps to realise his Godhood. All that he desires will automatically follow him."

2. Linda Goodman, Author, 'Star Signs'

- When the "Money Mystique" is ignored, whether through greed or the ignorance of the Law, the money gained either gradually dwindles away...... or is accumulated to the level of stagnation within the spirit of the one who hoards it, bringing all the accompanying miseries of the fear of loss. Money must not change hands between the esoteric teacher and student."

3. Brahmarshi Patriji

- "Money & Spirituality" seem like two different worlds. Hindus have a Goddess of Wealth—

'Mahalakshmi'. Money as such is to be revered as God, to be spent wisely by divine persons for divine purposes. That is the way of worshiping the Goddess Mahalakshmi. Goddess Lakshmi, money and spirituality form a perfect union. When all human beings attain such a perfect union in themselves, Earth will be a Heaven in an instant."

4. Thirukkural

- Verse 754:
  "Wealth acquired in thrift by fair means, goes to build virtue and bliss through contentment and satisfaction."

5. Santh Kabir Das

- Hindi Verse:
  Jab Man Laagaa Loabh Soan, Gayaa Vishaya mein Bhoye Kahain Kabir Vichaari Ke, Kehi Prakaar Dhan Hoye

  Saint Kabirdas contemplates and explains— When someone's mind is caught in the greed of wealth and riches, he, entangled in the clutches of worldly affairs, forgets his 'self', i.e., he does not see anything else. He keeps on contemplating day and night ways of accumulating riches'.

  Hindi Verse:
  Hum ghar jara apna, looka linha haath |
  Vahooka ghar phoonkhoon, jo chale hamare saath ||

Kabir Saheb indicates that he has snapped his worldly connections completely and that he would snap them for anyone who wants to join him. He implies that worldly attachments are impediments to following the true spiritual pursuits and should be snapped in order to embark on a real spiritual path that will give everlasting peace.

6. Osho Bhagwan Rajneesh (Abridged from 'The Book of Wisdom')

- "I will not tell you to renounce money. That has been told to you over the ages: it has not changed you. I am going to tell you something else: celebrate life, and obsession with money disappears automatically. And when it goes on its own accord, it leaves no scratches, it leaves no wounds behind, it leaves no trace behind."

Wisdom from Adi Sankaracharya

In his masterpiece, "Bhaja Govindam", Adi Sankaracharya highlights the importance of contentment in one's life if the seeker desires to enjoy his wealth and also live in harmony.

Sankaracharya's Vision: Not Renunciation of Life, but Liberation through Wisdom.

It is a common misunderstanding that Sri Adi Sankaracharya stood only for *vairagya* (renunciation). In truth, his was a holistic vision that did not deny life's joys but refined them through wisdom. He did not advocate running away from the world, but rising above its illusions. His emphasis was not on rejecting wealth, but on understanding its true place in life.

Wealth, in itself, is neither sinful nor condemned. It is not the possession of wealth, but the endless craving for more that binds and blinds the soul. The scriptures and sages never said, *"Renounce wealth,"* but rather, *"Renounce the thirst for wealth."* Use what comes to you as a result of your past meritorious actions (*punya karmas*) wisely and with contentment. Live in the world but do not be consumed by it.

Contentment (*santosha*) is the true wealth. Accept what life brings with gratitude, and let your mind rest in satisfaction. Do not allow your peace to be shaken by comparison, competition, or covetousness. Earn your living righteously (*dharma-artham*), without deceit, exploitation, or greed. Let your earnings be pure, and your life, peaceful.

Cleanse the mind of its clinging to possessions, pleasures, and passing things. Let go of the feverish attachment to the transient.

Then, you will not only survive in this world—you will truly live.

With a purified mind and an inwardly turned gaze, begin to contemplate that which is eternal, unchanging, and real—the Self, the *Atman*. Direct your energies toward the Supreme Truth that underlies all existence.

Such a life is not one of denial, but of true enjoyment. It is *vaibhoga*—a noble enjoyment rooted in detachment, discernment (*viveka*), and inner freedom. This alone leads to lasting happiness, peace, and ultimately, liberation (*moksha*).

Let your outer life be simple, your inner life be rich. In that lies the true message of Sankaracharya—a life of wisdom, balance, and spiritual fulfilment.

Powerful Questions for Self-Introspection

You can read each of these powerful questions which is a gateway to introspection and self- transformation. They help us realize what is most important in life. Mere reading them will guide us on our journey towards Self-Realization. You may answer them by yourself or also after discussing with family and friends.

You may write or type out your answers and ideas together with your insights.

1. What would you do if you had abundant money and working is not necessary?

2. What were your dreams when you were younger?

3. What do you think is impossible to do? (This question stimulates out-of-the-box thinking + highlights the limitations we really believe to be real)

4. What would you do if you win Rs.1 crore?

5. What would you do if today is the last day of your life?

6. What does success mean for you?

7. What do you admire most about others?

8.   What does success mean for you?

9.   How do you see life in 10 years?

10. If you were immortal, what would you do with your life?

It is recommended to remember these questions as they can change the course of superficial interactions and reveal the deeper aspirations of people we live and associate with.

May you live your highest life!!!

Annexure

How To Do Meditation?

RIGHT POSTURE

Sit comfortably—either on the floor, (or) on the chair, (or) on the sofa.

Clasp your hands, cross your feet.

If you are wearing glasses (spectacles), remove them, and gently close your eyes

OBSERVATION OF THE BREATH

Witness your simple, easy, tender, normal, Natural Breath.

When you're with your breath, your mind naturally becomes empty.

Whenever thoughts arise, immediately bring your attention back to your NATURAL BREATH.

COMPLETION OF MEDITATION

Unclasp your hands and place your fingers on your eyes for five seconds Gently open your eyes by slowly removing your fingers.

Benefits of Meditation

Benefits of Meditation are manifold :

- Mind naturally stays in **Peaceful** and **Joyful** state

- **Memory** power increases

- Wasteful **Habits** die naturally

- Diseases gets **Healed** faster

- **Efficiency** in all work increases

- Heightened **Awareness**
- Ability to **Discern** right and wrong gets sharpened
- **Willpower** and **Self-Esteem** naturally become stronger
- Interpersonal **Relationships** become qualitative and fulfilling
- **Purpose of Life** is thoroughly understood
- Life becomes **Celebration**

and, many more...

SOULFULL FEDERATION TRUST ®

Lord Buddha's clarion call to 'be a light unto oneself' encouraged him to set up an institution i.e., a Charitable Trust named SOULFULL FEDERATION TRUST® in the year 2018 to spiritualise and enlighten individuals about meditation,holistic living, etc. free of cost. More than 10,000 meditation sessions under the auspices of the trust have been conducted so far while the activity to publish and circulate spiritual wisdom has just taken roots. It is our earnest appeal to all spiritual seekers to support the mission of the trust by their donation.

Dhyāna Ratna S.K. Rajan
Chairman
Soulfull Federation Trust®

 **SOULFULL FEDERATION TRUST®**

.....springboard for enlightenment

About the Author —
Dhyāna Ratna S. K. Rajan

Dhyāna Ratna S. K. Rajan is a retired senior banker whose life took a profound spiritual turn after a series of transformative encounters with illumined souls and realised masters. These blessed interactions opened before him the deeper dimensions of life and awakened an inner call to tread the path of Dhyāna and Self-discovery. A seeker by temperament and a voracious reader by habit, he found his true joy in imbibing the timeless teachings of great sages and spiritual luminaries who have guided humanity across the ages.

At the gentle urging of revered spiritual mentors, he took to writing—so that the distilled wisdom of the Masters could be shared with earnest seekers every where. His works span a wide range of spiritual and self-elevating themes, drawing from the perennial teachings of Ādi Śaṅkarācārya, Gautama Buddha, Swami Sivanda and many other enlightened beings, as well as from insights on holistic living—encompassing physical, emotional, and mental purity. Through his writings, he aspires to rekindle in the reader a living spirituality—one that is not confined to ritual or tradition alone, but blossoms as a direct, heartfelt experience of the divine within.